IGNATIUS CRITICAL EDITIONS

Study Guide for *Moby-Dick*
— *by Herman Melville* —

Edited by
Mary R. Reichardt

Series Editor
Joseph Pearce

Introduction by
Patrick S. J. Carmack

IGNATIUS PRESS   SAN FRANCISCO

Cover design by John Herreid

© 2011 Ignatius Press, San Francisco
All rights reserved

ISBN 978-1-58617-417-0

Printed in the United States of America ∞

Table of Contents

Why a Great Books Study Guide? 5

How to Use This Guide 11

Context 13

Bare Bones: The Skeleton Plot 15

Words Made Flesh: Summary of Critical Appraisals and Study Questions 18

    Mary R. Reichardt: "'A Large and Liberal Theme': An Introduction to *Moby-Dick*" 18

    Herman Melville: Excerpts from "Hawthorne and His Mosses" 19

    Robert Alexander: "Apocalyptic Readings of *Moby-Dick*: What Ishmael Returns to Tell Us" 19

    Mitchell Kalpakgian: "'Civilized Hypocrisies and Bland Deceits' in *Moby-Dick*" 20

    Stephen Zelnick: "*Moby-Dick*: The Republic at Sea" 21

Things to Think About While Reading the Book 23

Study Questions on the Text of *Moby-Dick* 25

    Part One—Knowledge of the Text 25

    Part Two—Essay Questions 27

Answer Key for *Moby-Dick* 33

Why a Great Books Study Guide?

Wisdom is generally acknowledged to be the highest good of the human mind, whether this be recognized as knowledge of first principles and causes or as a contemplative gaze at Wisdom itself. But how does one obtain wisdom? The means is primarily conversation with great and wise persons who have already advanced far along the paths of knowledge and understanding to wisdom. As the philosopher Dr. Peter Redpath succinctly puts it when addressing audiences of young people interested in understanding why they ought to read great books, "If you wish to become wise, learn from wise people."

Since, however, persons of great wisdom are rare and generally unavailable to us due to distance or death, we enter into conversation with them through their books which record their thought. In doing this, we soon discover how all the authors of great books used this same method of study themselves. They began by conversing with or reading the great books written by the sages of earlier generations. In so doing, they avoided having to re-invent the wheel each generation; and they avoided making mistakes already dealt with and were able to build on existing foundations. Indeed what would be the point in studying mediocre works by lesser luminaries or beginning all thought over from square one every few years, when great books by the wisest people—the great sages of civilization—are readily available?

> The reading of all good books is indeed like a conversation with the noblest men of past centuries who were the authors of them, nay a carefully studied conversation, in which they reveal to us none but the best of their thoughts. (Rene Descartes, *Discourse on Method*)

Through the internal dialectical process found in the great books—the references, discussions, critiques, and responses to the thought of the authors' wise predecessors, a process referred to as the "Great Conversation" by Robert M. Hutchins—we may closely follow the development of the investigations conducted by these wise men into the great ideas they have pondered and about which they have written. This manner of study has always been the normative approach to wisdom in the West.

> Until lately the West has regarded it as self-evident that the road to education lay through great books. No man was educated until he was acquainted with the masterpieces of his tradition. . . . They were the principal instruments of liberal education. . . . The goal toward which Western society moves is the Civilization of the Dialogue. The spirit of Western civilization is the spirit of inquiry. Its dominant element is *Logos*.[1]

No ongoing dialogue comparable in duration or breadth exists in the East. Pope Benedict XVI has mentioned that Western civilization has become the dominant civilization because of its closer correspondence to human nature. In his 2006 Regensburg lecture, he noted that there exists a real analogy between our created reason and God, who is *Logos* (meaning both "reason" and "word"). To abandon reason—and hence the dialogue, which is both reason's natural expression and necessary aid—would be contrary both to the nature of man and of God. This cumulative wisdom of the West is preserved and transmitted in its great music and art, but most particularly in the study of its great books which record the results of three millennia of dialogue, guided by reason, concerning the most profound ideas with which we must all grapple such as existence, life, love, happiness, and so forth.

---

[1] Robert M. Hutchins, *The Great Conversation: The Substance of a Liberal Education*, vol. 1, *The Great Books of the Western World* (Chicago: Encyclopedia Britannica, Inc., 1952).

This manner of learning is greatly facilitated when the reader also engages in a dialectic exchange—a live conversation (in person or now online)—with other readers of the same books, probing and discussing the great ideas contained in them and, one hopes, carrying them a few steps further. This method of learning is often referred to as the Socratic method, after the ancient Athenian philosopher Socrates, who initiated its use as a deliberate way to obtain understanding and wisdom through mutual inquiry and discussion. This same "questioning" method was used by Christ, who often answered questions with other questions, parables, and stories that left the hearers wondering, questioning, and thinking. He already knew the answers, as Socrates often did. The goal was not merely indoctrination of the memory with information, facts, and knowledge, but mind- and life-changing understanding and wisdom.

This study guide is intended for students (if one is still learning, one is a student) who have read—extensively—lesser works, particularly the classic children's literature. Given that degree of preparation, students of high school age and older, including adults, can pick up Homer's *Iliad* and *Odyssey* or Herodotus' *Histories* and other great works and enter into the seminal thought of the most influential books of our culture and civilization. There is reason not to delay such education.

The great books are, for the most part, the most interesting and well written of all books. They were not written for experts. Their wide and enduring appeal to generation after generation testifies to that fact. Readers reasonably prepared for them will find them captivating, entertaining, and enlightening. Naturally, some readers will profit more than others from the great books, but all will profit from learning about the Trojan War, ancient civilizations, the heroes of ancient Greece, the early tragedies, and the thought of Aristotle. Works such as Genesis, the *Aeneid*, Saint Augustine's *Confessions*, Chaucer's *Canterbury Tales*, Dante's *Divine Comedy*, Saint Thomas Aquinas' *Summa theologica*, and Shakespeare's plays are foundational for and/or profoundly influential on our way of life. These works are essential for participation in the Great Conversation mentioned above. The enduring intellectual dialogue begins with the works of Homer, the "father of civilization", and proceeds through the centuries, eventually absorbing the Old and New Testaments in a lengthy reformulation of classical civilization into Western civilization, which continues—albeit always under assault by various errors—right up to our time.

The principal guides in selecting the works of enduring appeal to be included in the corpus of great books, besides generations of readers, include the late, great Dr. Mortimer J. Adler, who worked for eighty years (from 1921 to 2000, when I had the privilege to participate in his last Socratic discussion groups) to restore and keep the great classics, including particularly those by Plato, Aristotle, and Aquinas, in the Western canon of great books. As Dr. Adler put it, "The great books constitute the backbone of a liberal education." But read alone in our postmodernist context of radical skepticism, the great books can easily be misunderstood and used for all manner of mischief. It was precisely a desire to provide a deeper understanding of the importance and influence of the great books—to highlight what is true and great in them and to expose and defang what is false—that inspired Ignatius Press to initiate its important Critical Editions series.

Augmenting the work of Dr. Adler, on behalf of Ignatius Press, is Joseph Pearce, the author of several critically acclaimed, best-selling biographies of great authors, who has diligently worked as the author and/or editor of these study guides to accompany the Ignatius Critical Editions, of which he is also the series editor. Our gratitude extends to Father Joseph Fessio for his encouragement of this much-needed project, which is so broad in scope and vision as to be potentially revolutionary in the schools, colleges, and universities dominated by relativism. Homeschoolers, though somewhat shielded from the relativism of the schools, will find in these guides a welcome and trustworthy means of introduction to the great books and to their careful and critical reading.

Finally, it is worth emphasizing that these Ignatius Critical Editions Study Guides are merely introductory guides with tests, questions, and answer keys helpful for student assessment. The great books themselves are the primary texts, their authors our primary teachers.

Patrick S. J. Carmack
January 18, 2008

Patrick S. J. Carmack, J.D., is the president of the Great Books Academy Homeschool Program (greatbooksacademy.org), the Angelicum Academy Homeschool Program (angelicum.net), the Western Civilization Foundation, and the online publication *Classical Homeschooling Magazine* (classicalhomeschooling.com).

How to Use This Guide

The Ignatius Critical Editions (ICE) Study Guides are intended to assist students and teachers in their reading of the Ignatius Critical Editions. Each guide gives a short introductory appraisal of the contextual factors surrounding the writing of the literary work, a short "bare bones" summary of the plot, and a more in-depth summary of some of the essential critical aspects of the work. There is also a list of things to think about while reading the book, designed to focus the reader's critical faculties. These points to ponder will enable the reader to rise above a merely recreational reading of the text to a level of critical and literary appreciation befitting the work itself.

Finally, there are questions for the student to answer. These fall into two distinct categories: questions concerned with a knowledge of the *facts* of the work, and questions concerned with analyzing the *truths* that emerge from the work. This approach is rooted in the fundamental axiom, taught by great philosophers such as Aristotle and Saint Thomas Aquinas, that we must go *through* the facts *to* the truth. Put simply, an inadequate knowledge of the facts of a work (who did what and when, who said what to whom, etc.) will inevitably lead to a failure to understand the work on its deeper levels of meaning.

As such, readers of the work are strongly encouraged to answer all the *fact-related* questions in part 1. The close reading of the text that this will entail will prepare them for the essay questions in part 2. With regard to the latter, it is left to the discretion of the teacher (or the reader) as to how many of these questions should be answered. Some of the questions, particularly those calling for a contextual reading of the work in relation to other works, might be unsuitable for less-advanced students or readers. In such cases, the teacher (or reader) should use his discretion in deciding which of the essay questions should be answered. In any event, you have been provided with an abundance of questions from which to choose!

Teachers should also be aware that the answer key can be removed before the study guide is made available to the student. Answers to the questions in the "Bare Bones" and "Things to Think About" sections are not included in the answer key because these questions are intended to raise issues for the student to ponder and are not intended to be employed for examination purposes.

It should be noted that the Ignatius Critical Editions and the ICE Study Guides approach these great works of literature from a tradition-oriented perspective. Those seeking deconstruction, "queer theory", feminism, postcolonialism, and other manifestations of the latest academic fads and fashions will be disappointed. If you are unable to think outside the postmodern box, this guide is not for you!

Context

Early in *Moby-Dick* the narrator Ishmael tells us, "[A] whale-ship was my Yale College and my Harvard" (see *Moby-Dick*, p. 152), and throughout his writings Herman Melville capitalized on his youthful experiences at sea. Born in New York City in 1819 to a prosperous merchant family, he tried a variety of jobs after his father's business collapsed in 1830, thrusting the family into relative poverty. At the age of nineteen he shipped as an apprentice on the merchant vessel *St. Lawrence* bound for Liverpool. After a brief stint at schoolteaching back in New York, he embarked on his first whaling voyage in 1841 aboard the *Acushnet*, which sailed from New Bedford, Massachusetts, for the South Seas. Eighteen months later, a poor catch and a quarrelsome captain led him and a fellow sailor to desert ship on the Marquesas Islands. From there Melville shipped again on another whaler, the *Lucy Ann*, but soon mutinied with others and was put ashore in Tahiti. He next sailed briefly on his third and last whaler, the *Charles and Henry*. After clerking for a time at a store in Honolulu, he enlisted in the U.S. Navy and sailed home on the frigate *United States*. He returned to New York State in 1844, where his family, now in better financial condition, was living at Lansingburgh. Urged by relatives to write down stories of his adventures, he produced his first book, *Typee*, in 1846, an account of his stay among the primitive Taipis tribe of the Marquesas. The book was an immediate best seller, and Melville followed it with *Omoo* (1847), a second South Seas adventure tale. That year, at the age of twenty-eight, he married Elizabeth Shaw. Several years later he moved his family from New York City to a farm he called Arrowhead near Pittsfield, New York. Meanwhile, the 1849 *Mardi*, a philosophical satire, was not successful, and reluctantly Melville returned to his "potboiler" sea stories, publishing *Redburn* (1849) and *White-Jacket* (1850).

Several events occurred around the year 1850 leading to the exceptionally fertile period that produced *Moby-Dick*. Melville had most likely begun the story of Ishmael's voyage on the Pequod when he met Nathaniel Hawthorne, whose work he greatly admired for its profundity. The "shock of recognition" of a fellow author whose artistic goals seemed similar to his own renewed his determination to write what he felt compelled to write despite the possibility of failure.[1] The 1851 *Moby-Dick*, combining a whaling adventure with layers of metaphysical speculation, baffled his readers. The following year, *Pierre*, an exploration of the complexities of human behavior, sealed his reputation as an impenetrable author. Melville wrote little during the remainder of his life, although some of his later writings, such as "Bartleby the Scrivener", "Benito Cereno", and the posthumous *Billy Budd*, are among his best works. For nearly twenty years he earned his living as customs inspector at the port of New York. He died in 1891. Rediscovered in the 1920s, *Moby-Dick* is now considered an American masterpiece.

---

[1] Herman Melville, "Hawthorne and His Mosses", in *Moby-Dick*, by Herman Melville, a Norton Critical Edition, eds. Harrison Hayford and Hershel Parker (New York: W. W. Norton, 1967), p. 547.

Bare Bones: The Skeleton Plot

The plot of *Moby-Dick* is quite slender, for it is only the scaffolding for the philosophic inquiry that makes up the bulk of the work. Although the famous line "Call me Ishmael" begins the narrative proper, the first two characters we meet are the "pale Usher", or assistant schoolteacher, who gives us an etymology of the word "whale", and the "sub-sub-librarian", who provides several pages of extracts from a wide variety of sources concerning the whale. Next appears the enigmatic narrator Ishmael, who, we learn, is relating his experience from some years earlier. In a state of near-suicidal depression, he decides to go to sea on a whaling adventure, partly to cure his blues but also to attempt to grasp "the ungraspable phantom of life" by taking such a risk, something, he believes, all deep-thinking people should do (see *Moby-Dick*, p. 31). Arriving in New Bedford, Massachusetts, he seeks a room in the Spouter-Inn but is told he must share a bed with a strange South Seas harpooner. His fears nearly confirmed by Queequeg's tattooed body and pagan idol worship, Ishmael nevertheless soon comes to respect the savage's courteous and kindly manner, and the two become close friends. After hearing a sermon at the Whaleman's Chapel by Father Mapple on the Old Testament figure of Jonah, Ishmael and Queequeg go to Nantucket, where they sign onto the Pequod, negotiating their salary or particular "lay" with the ship's owners, Captains Peleg and Bildad. Even after learning that the Pequod's unfortunately named captain, Ahab, is an odd man who has had his leg taken off in a previous voyage by a whale, the jocular Ishmael brushes off this and other ominous signs, such as the persistent warnings of a gaunt man, Elijah.

The Pequod sets sail on Christmas Day, but it is not until some time into the voyage that Captain Ahab finally appears on deck. With his whalebone leg and long white scar, he is a startling and imposing figure. For the first time, the Pequod's crew learns that the money-making whaling voyage they had signed on to is but a sham, a cover for Ahab's true mission—to hunt down the great white whale, Moby Dick, that has maimed him. Nailing a gold doubloon to a mast, Ahab bribes the crew with the promise of the reward going to the first man who spots the whale. He rallies them to his demonic purpose by a kind of solidarity built of mass hysteria, staging a ritual in which the three pagan harpooners, Queequeg, Tashtego, and Dagoo, temper their lances with blood and pledge themselves to the hunt. Only the stalwart first mate, the Quaker Christian Starbuck, opposes Ahab's intent, but his several attempts to sway the monomaniacal captain from his purpose prove ineffectual.

Although "Ahab has his humanities" (see *Moby-Dick*, p. 118), one by one they drop away, including his pipe and the quadrant, as he relentlessly pursues the white whale. When the Pequod encounters its first shoal of whales, shadowy figures that Ahab has smuggled aboard—his private harpooners, including the sinister Parsee Fedallah—emerge from the hold. Fedallah predicts that Ahab will die in the struggle to kill Moby Dick—two hearses will proceed him, the second of which will be made from American wood, and he will be killed by hemp—but Ahab dismisses this dark prophecy, preferring to consider himself immortal.

As the ship sails on, it captures a few whales, and Ishmael, whose voice increasingly becomes one with the crew, details every aspect of capturing, killing, and processing whales. These "whale matter" chapters are interspersed between the dramatic chapters that advance the plot. The ever-meditating Ishmael also considers every angle of the whaling business; whales in history, mythology, and art; whale behavior; and, of course, the mystery of the albino whale, Moby Dick. Always given to paradoxes and ambiguities, he frequently draws morals from his meditations. As the ship sails on, the plot is also punctuated by a series of meetings, or "gams", that the Pequod has with other whaling ships. Several of these encounters, such as that with the *Jeroboam*, the *Samuel Enderby*, the *Rachel*, and the *Delight*, indicate that the Pequod is getting closer to Moby Dick. Meanwhile, the daily hazards of life on a whaleship continue. At one point, the harpooner Tashtego falls into an excavated whale's head and is rescued from a terrible death by Queequeg. The little black boy, Pip, goes insane after being nearly abandoned in the sea by men more intent on the whale catch than on his rescue. Still later, Queequeg grows ill and has the ship carpenter make him a coffin, but he later recovers.

Finally, it is Ahab himself who spots Moby Dick. For two days, the Pequod's crew struggles with the enormous whale as it destroys the boats sent after it. On the third day, the whale kills Ahab—just as Fedallah had predicted—and rams the Pequod so that the ship and crew sink into its vortex-like wake. Only Ishmael, clinging to Queequeg's coffin, survives to tell the story.

Words Made Flesh: Summary of Critical Appraisals and Study Questions

The questions posed in this section are not intended for examination purposes but are designed to prompt appropriate trains of thought for the student to ponder as he reads the work. Questions intended for examination purposes are to be found in the "Study Questions on the Text" at the end of the study guide.

Mary R. Reichardt: "'A Large and Liberal Theme': An Introduction to *Moby-Dick*"

Melville capitalized on his early experiences at sea in much of his writing. Although readers applauded his realistic sea adventure stories, such as *Typee* and *Redburn*, his desire to capture "truth" in his writings led to *Moby-Dick*'s decidedly mixed reviews and overall financial failure. The truth Melville wished to express may be seen in the context of the transcendental Romantic idealism then in vogue. Against the naïve optimism of such a philosophy, Melville wrote a novel that expresses the "power of blackness" (see Melville, excerpts from "Hawthorne and His Mosses", p. 654) in the similar "monomanias" of the characters Ahab and Ishmael. Ultimately, Melville expresses a tragic view of unbridled American individualism.

1. What are some of the events and experiences that led up to Melville's writing of *Moby-Dick*?

2. According to Reichardt, what is the "truth" Melville wished to capture in *Moby-Dick*? How does it reflect his Calvinist heritage?

3. How might Ishmael's statement about Narcissus being "the key to it all" (see *Moby-Dick*, p. 31) apply to both Ahab and Ishmael?

Herman Melville: Excerpts from "Hawthorne and His Mosses"

This piece by Melville, although a review of Hawthorne's 1846 short-story collection *Mosses from an Old Manse*, has long been considered a window into Melville's own artistic aspirations. In it, he famously describes Hawthorne as a deceptively benign author who in reality exhibits a "power of blackness" that "derives its force from its appeals to that Calvinistic sense of Innate Depravity and Original Sin". He compares Hawthorne to Shakespeare in his quest for truth, and he calls for a uniquely American literature: "But it is better to fail in originality, than to succeed in imitation."

1. How does Melville describe the "power of blackness" he sees in Hawthorne's stories? What is the effect of this "blackness"?

2. Melville knew he would surprise his readers by comparing Hawthorne to Shakespeare. Why does he do so?

3. In what ways does Melville call for a uniquely American literature?

4. What concepts from this review might apply to Melville's own writing of *Moby-Dick*?

Robert Alexander: "Apocalyptic Readings of *Moby-Dick*: What Ishmael Returns to Tell Us"

Moby-Dick repeatedly raises questions about how we read. In the novel, Melville attempts to deal with the clash between two different ways of "reading the world": a scientific, rationalist way and a biblical, faith-based way. One way to read is for theme: Melville's novel is a sustained critique of New England Christianity and the hypocrisy and cupidity of human nature. Another way to read is for character. Ahab exhibits an internal struggle between his Protestant upbringing and a rationalist modern mind-set: he strikes out at the cold indifference of nature and his apparently purposeless suffering. With Ishmael we have the problem of reading a character who is both actor and narrator. In a third way of reading, we grasp the poetic form of the book, which centers on Ishmael's role as a Jonah figure. What he brings back—the book itself and its accruing Christian images—points to the need for humility in reading the universe correctly and the central place of the Cross.

1. According to this essay, in what ways does *Moby-Dick* criticize New England Christianity?

2. According to Alexander, in what ways is Ahab spiritually conflicted due to his Protestant upbringing and his rationalist-scientific mind-set? What admirable qualities does he possess?

3. "The difficulty in grasping Ishmael's role in the plot's forward motion is that he conducts two interlinking lines of action." Explain this point.

4. Alexander maintains that the "germ" of the novel is Ishmael's role as a Jonah figure. According to the essay, what does Ishmael bring back to readers? How does the novel point toward Christ's Cross?

Mitchell Kalpakgian: "'Civilized Hypocrisies and Bland Deceits' in *Moby-Dick*"

Moby-Dick concerns a sea expedition that quickly goes beyond a typical whaling voyage for profit and assumes a moral and spiritual dimension. The clash between Ahab and Moby Dick represents the eternal conflict between good and evil, with evil ever present and lurking just beneath surface reality despite human attempts to ignore, cover, or deny it. Thus the novel becomes a profound metaphysical drama. Although Ishmael enlists on the Pequod as an idealistic seaman in search of adventure, he is soon immersed in this world of evil and initiated into the "civilized hypocrisies and bland deceits" of surface appearances that attempt to mask it. Like the voracious sharks that ominously swim just below the calm and lovely surface of the sea, the whaling voyage as a whole, according to Kalpakgian, "brings men down to earth from idle daydreaming and philosophic gazing to the realities of death and evil that lie below in the hidden chambers of the soul".

1. In what ways, according to Kalpakgian, does Ishmael come to realize the "civilized hypocrisies and bland deceits" that cover the evil hiding just below the surface?

2. How is the natural world deceptive, especially as seen in chapter 42, "The Whiteness of the Whale"?

3. How do the "civilized hypocrisies and bland deceits" that Melville exposes in the novel reflect a commentary on mid-nineteenth-century American culture?

4. How does the whale itself "reveal aspects of evil that constantly threaten mankind"?

5. "In the final chapters, all law and order and right reason collapse." Explain what Kalpakgian means by this statement.

Stephen Zelnick: "*Moby-Dick*: The Republic at Sea"

Melville shares with thinkers throughout the ages worries about the shortcomings of democracy, and *Moby-Dick* may thus be seen as an extended meditation on the subject. Using Alexis de Tocqueville's 1835 *Democracy in America*, this essay looks at de Tocqueville's observations on the American democratic experiment, especially the threat of tyranny, to which an inexperienced population naïvely promoting unrestrained liberty was particularly susceptible. In the microcosm of a "world at sea"—the diverse crew of the Pequod—and in the jocular "anarchist" Ishmael, Melville explores how Ahab, a master politician, skillfully yet easily manipulates his crew and wields dictatorial power. Even Starbuck, the lone "aristocrat" on board, succumbs to Ahab's monomaniacal control. Thus, according to Zelnick, "*Moby-Dick* tells us more about the embattled American experiment in liberty and democracy than most have chosen to recognize."

1. Why did de Tocqueville have concerns about American democracy? What were those concerns?

2. In what way is Ishmael a "happy anarchist" who "despises authority"? What are the consequences of such attitudes?

3. What four reasons does Zelnick give for Ahab's being able to achieve tyranny over his crew?

4. "In fact, the tragic figure in *Moby-Dick* is not Ahab but the quietly tormented Starbuck." Explain this statement.

5. How, according to Zelnick, does Father Mapple's sermon contribute to a spirit of "excess and narcissism, not to law, to constitutional traditions, or to cultural conventions that support a vigorous republic"?

Things to Think About While Reading the Book

The questions posed in this section are not intended for examination purposes but are designed to prompt appropriate trains of thought for the student to ponder as he reads the work. Questions intended for examination purposes are to be found in the "Study Questions on the Text" at the end of the study guide.

1. *Moby-Dick* seems an uneven novel in several ways. The narrator, Ishmael, dominates the first chapters, but once on board the Pequod, he becomes "one of that crew" in supporting Ahab's quest (see *Moby-Dick*, p. 226); consequently, we "lose" his distinctive voice as the plot concerning Ahab takes over. As you read, consider whether or not the novel suffers from this uneven tone and form or whether these are integral to the book's overall themes.

2. *Moby-Dick* is a novel about epistemology: the study of how we know what we know. In dissecting the physical whale, in detailing the whale's habitats and habits, in exploring the whale in literature and myth, Ishmael tells us all a person could possibly *know* about the whale. But, in the end, what do we really *know*? It is here that Melville makes use of the book of Job and God's answer to Job about trying to understand what is too great for human comprehension. As you read the novel, consider what it says about the limitations of human knowledge in the face of the mysteries of the universe.

3. Like his friend Nathaniel Hawthorne, Melville was interested in exploring what he called "the power of blackness", that which "derives its force from its appeals to that Calvinistic sense of Innate Depravity and Original Sin, from whose visitations . . . no deeply thinking mind is always and wholly free" (see Melville, excerpts from "Hawthorne and His Mosses", p. 654). As such, *Moby-Dick* is a profound study of evil, both real and perceived, in the cosmos and in the heart of mankind. Countering the transcendental idealists such as Ralph Waldo Emerson and Henry David Thoreau who advocated "self-reliance", Melville explores the "dark necessity" in human nature that can drive humans to evil and result in such a monomaniacal, unbalanced tyrant as Captain Ahab. As you read, consider how the novel explores the existence of evil in the universe and in the human heart.

4. The ever-philosophizing Ishmael often dwells on the many contradictions of life. A strong sense of the ambiguous and paradoxical nature of the cosmos and the relativity of human perception permeates his musings. Life is a paradox, full of unsolvable contradictions: for example, the interplay between free will and determinism and between good and evil; the fact that a pagan cannibal makes a better friend than a sober Christian; and the fact that the precious substance ambergris is found in a dead, decaying whale. As you read, consider how Ishmael continues to emphasize the universe's contradictions and paradoxes. Note too how the novel emphasizes the relative nature of human perception in such chapters as "The Whiteness of the Whale" (chap. 42) and "The Doubloon" (chap. 99).

5. As you finish the novel, consider why Melville appended an epigraph from the book of Job to the epilogue: "And I only am escaped alone to tell thee." What, finally, does Ishmael want to tell us? Does the book contain a single "moral" or meaning, or is such a summary statement impossible?

Study Questions on the Text of *Moby-Dick*

Part One—Knowledge of the Text

1. What are the names of the three mates of the Pequod?

2. "I'll try a pagan friend, thought I, since Christian kindness has proved but hollow courtesy." Who says these words, and about whom?

3. What kind of food is served at the Try-Pots in Nantucket?

4. With what is the Pequod decorated?

5. Describe Queequeg's "Ramadan".

6. Who is Elijah?

7. What is the main theme of Father Mapple's sermon?

8. On what day does the Pequod sail?

9. Who is called a "a grand, ungodly, god-like man"?

10. Who are Captains Bildad and Peleg, and what religion do they profess?

11. Who is Bulkington, and what does he symbolize to Ishmael?

12. Besides his loss of a leg, what other physical feature is immediately noticeable in Ahab?

13. What does Ahab hammer onto the mainmast, promising it as a reward to the first person to sight Moby Dick?

14. "Vengeance on a dumb brute . . . that simply smote thee from blindest instinct! Madness! To be enraged with a dumb thing, Captain Ahab, seems blasphemous." Who says this?

15. Who is Fedallah?

16. What is a gam?

17. Who are Steelkilt and Radney, and what happens to them?

18. In the gam with the *Jeroboam*, what is mad Gabriel's warning to Ahab?

19. Who falls into a whale's head and nearly drowns?

20. What is ambergris, and where is it to be found?

21. What happens to Pip?

22. What does Ahab see in the three peaks on the doubloon? What does Starbuck see?

23. What limb has Captain Boomer of the *Samuel Enderby* lost to Moby Dick?

24. What is the ship *Rachel* searching for?

25. As the lone survivor of the Pequod, Ishmael is buoyed up by what item as he awaits rescue?

Part Two—Essay Questions

1. Describe the changing character of Ishmael as we see him in the book's early chapters; as he grows in experience on the Pequod; and finally (after approximately chapter 96, "The Try-Works") as the book's plot shifts toward Ahab. Do you agree, as some have noted, that we essentially "lose" Ishmael as the book progresses? If so, why would Melville have done this?

2. What is the main moral or lesson that Father Mapple draws from the book of Jonah in his sermon, and how can the framework of both the book of Jonah and the book of Job be applied to the novel's themes? In particular, consider why in the epilogue Ishmael gives us as epigraph the repeated cry of those who brings Job news of disaster: "And I only am escaped alone to tell thee." What, finally, does Ishmael wish to tell us?

3. Consider the novel's many chapters on "whale matter"—facts and stories concerning whales and whaling. These begin with chapter 24, "The Advocate". Why is Ishmael so concerned with detailing all the world's knowledge about whales and whaling? How does this intermittent concentration on whales contribute to the book's themes about the quest for knowledge? Increasingly, Ishmael notes the many ironies and ambiguities associated with whales and whaling. In your discussion, consider at least several of these ironies and ambiguities and how Ishmael uses them analogically to point to some aspect of human life in the cosmos.

4. Reread chapters 36 through 40, and also 46. Here, Ahab reveals his diabolical mission and rallies the crew's support. How does Ahab manage to muster his crew around his purpose by careful manipulation? What is the crew's response? Why do you suppose Melville begins here to present some chapters, such as 38, 39, and 40, like a play, with stage directions, soliloquies, and so forth?

5. Note carefully the early chapters, such as chapter 10, "A Bosom Friend", and chapter 11, "Nightgown", where Ishmael and Queequeg form a close relationship, and later chapters that concern human affection, connection, and bonding, such as chapter 72, "The Monkey-rope", and chapter 94, "A Squeeze of the Hand". Read Nathaniel Hawthorne's short story "Ethan Brand" and then relate the above chapters to (1) Hawthorne's conclusions in "Ethan Brand" about the "magnetic chain of humanity" and the consequences of separating oneself from it, and (2) Ahab's casting away of his pipe (chap. 30) and quadrant (chap. 118) and the successive loss of his "humanities" (see *Moby-Dick*, p. 118).

6. Both before and during the Pequod's voyage, ominous signs and prophecies abound. Make a list of these and then choose several to explore in depth. What does the sign or prophecy point to, and why? How is it fulfilled in the Pequod's tragic end?

7. Describe in full the three mates, Starbuck, Stubb, and Flask. What general type of humanity or kind of philosophy does each represent? Describe several scenes in which their given character traits are borne out.

8. Beginning with chapter 52, "The Pequod meets the Albatross", a series of gams intersperse the narrative. Describe each gam in sequence. Discuss how each meeting bears on the main story at hand—Ahab and his monomaniacal quest for Moby Dick—and note any emerging pattern that appears throughout the gams. How, especially, does the final ship, the *Delight*, comment ironically on Father Mapple's sermon about "delight" and "woe" in chapter 9?

9. Discuss Ahab as a tragic character, especially in his overweening pride and self-awareness.

10. Reread chapter 96, "The Try-Works". This chapter is often considered the climax or center of the book. What happens to Ishmael in this chapter, and what is his conclusion? What is Ishmael's point when he says that "there is a wisdom that is woe; but there is a woe that is madness" and mentions the "Catskill eagle" (see *Moby-Dick*, p. 495), and how do these conclusions relate to Ahab or the novel's themes as a whole? How do they relate to the theme developed by Solomon in the book of Ecclesiastes and to Father Mapple's sermon on "woe" versus "delight"?

11. Chapter 54, "The Town Ho's Story", is a long interpolated tale that Melville wrote for separate publication. In the figures of Steelkilt and Radney, how does the story provide a kind of microcosm of, or comment on, the tension between Starbuck and Ahab and the situation on the Pequod?

12. Along with his theme about the many contradictions and paradoxes of the universe, Melville dwells frequently in *Moby-Dick* on the subjectivity of human perception, that is, how it is often impossible to know the "truth" given that everyone has a different perception of that truth. Focus on chapter 99, "The Doubloon", in exploring this topic. What does each crew member see in the doubloon, and how does it reflect his personalities, philosophies, or goals?

13. Describe in full the character of Starbuck, the first mate. To the last, he pleads with Ahab to cease the quest for Moby Dick. Trace his encounters with Ahab throughout the novel, and draw a conclusion as to why his "mere unaided virtue" (see *Moby-Dick*, p. 234) is, finally, ineffective. Pay close attention to such moments as when Ahab gives in to him (chapter 109) and when Starbuck has a chance to kill or at least subdue Ahab and thus save the voyage (chapter 123). Is he right in not taking action against Ahab when he has the chance?

14. According to the novel, is Ahab's diabolic quest determined by forces outside of him? Or does he have free will? To answer this question, consider all we know and see about Ahab throughout the novel. What choices does he consciously make, and why? In what ways does he consider his fate determined? What, finally, does Melville conclude about Ahab's culpability for the tragic end of the Pequod? Is Ahab a sympathetic character at all?

15. In the character of Captain Ahab, *Moby-Dick* seems to speak about the ruthlessness and destruction of total self-reliance and absolute exertion of power. It seems to indicate that one must strike a balance between "head" and "heart" and, for sanity's sake, remain connected with the rest of humanity. In what ways does Ishmael manage to do this? He tells us in chapter 1 that the story of Narcissus "is the key to it all" (see *Moby-Dick*, p. 31). What does he mean by this? You may also wish to consider how *Moby-Dick* responds to Emerson, Thoreau, and mid-nineteenth-century transcendental idealistic notions of self-reliance.

16. One of *Moby-Dick*'s themes concerns the limitation of human knowledge, especially in the face of the mysteries of the universe and of human suffering. Ahab states that he hates and hunts down the whale for its "inscrutable" aspect, that is, that which he cannot understand (see *Moby-Dick*, p. 208). Ishmael, however, approaches the scope and limitation of human knowledge in a very different way, as revealed throughout the story that he tells us. In what ways does Ishmael try to understand the mysteries of the universe and, in particular, the mysterious leviathan? What, by contrast, is Ahab's technique? Can the novel be said to contain a "moral" in regard to this theme?

17. In what ways might the novel be considered an American epic? Comment, for example, on the work's use of American

settings, characters, idiom, traditions, religion, history, and so forth, as well as the industry of whaling, to describe the universal; to describe how the novel mingles the spiritual or supernatural realm with the natural; and to describe how the Pequod, in its diverse crew and precarious sea voyage, represents a microcosm of all humanity.

18. Through Ishmael, *Moby-Dick* frequently tells us that we must leave the shore and venture out to sea to be deep-thinking, fully alive people. "[B]etter is it to perish in that howling infinite, than be ingloriously dashed upon the lee, even if that were safety!" Ishmael tells us in the brief chapter on the fate of Bulkington (chapter 23, "The Lee Shore"; see *Moby-Dick*, p. 147). But is this true? Does the book—or, in your opinion, the more experienced Ishmael—still hold to this philosophy, given the novel's tragic end?

Answer Key for *Moby-Dick*

Note to Teachers: This answer key can be removed before the study guide is given to the student.

STUDY QUESTIONS

Part One—Knowledge of the Text

1. Starbuck, Stubb, and Flask
2. Ishmael says these words about Queequeg.
3. Chowder
4. Whale bones
5. He squats in the inn bedroom all day and night with the idol Yojo on his head.
6. A strange, shabby man who follows Ishmael and Queequeg and warns them about Ahab in dark and obscure terms
7. The disobedience, then repentance, of the biblical Jonah
8. Christmas Day
9. Captain Ahab
10. They are the Pequod's owners, and they are Quakers.
11. Bulkington is a newly landed whaleman who ships out immediately again on the Pequod. Ishmael sees him as a symbol of deep thinking and the restless pursuit of truth.
12. A long white scar running down his face and body
13. A gold doubloon

14. Starbuck
15. One of the shadowy harpooners that Ahab has stowed away and who emerge at the first sight of whales. Fedallah predicts Ahab's death.
16. A social meeting between whaleships at sea for the exchange of letters and news of whale sightings
17. Steelkilt and Radney are two whalemen aboard the *Town-Ho*. Steelkilt rebels against the mate Radney and is punished. He then plans to murder Radney, but Radney is killed by Moby Dick before Steelkilt can do so.
18. "Beware of the blasphemer's end!"
19. Tashtego
20. Ambergris is a soft, waxy substance found in the bowels of sick whales and used for making perfume.
21. He falls out of the boat as it goes after whales, is left alone in the sea for a time, and goes insane.
22. Ahab sees Ahab; Starbuck sees the Trinity.
23. His arm
24. The captain's young son
25. Queequeg's coffin

Part Two—Essay Questions

1. *Describe the changing character of Ishmael as we see him in the book's early chapters; as he grows in experience on the Pequod; and finally (after approximately chapter 96, "The Try-Works") as the book's plot shifts toward Ahab. Do you agree, as some have noted, that we essentially "lose" Ishmael as the book progresses? If so, why would Melville have done this?*

    Similar to that other great American classic, *Adventures of Huckleberry Finn*, *Moby-Dick* is uneven in tone and sometimes inconsistent in content. The quirky and buoyant Ishmael dominates the narrative in the early chapters but later, by his own admission ("I, Ishmael, was one of that crew" [see *Moby-Dick*, p. 226]), ominously blends with those who rally to Ahab's mission. In a larger view, the change in Ishmael may be considered integral to the novel's main themes. Your answer to this question should describe the Ishmael we see in the early part of the novel, in the middle, and in the end, and draw a conclusion about his character development.

2. *What is the main moral or lesson that Father Mapple draws from the book of Jonah in his sermon, and how can the framework of both the book of Jonah and the book of Job be applied to the novel's themes? In particular, consider why in the epilogue Ishmael gives us as epigraph the repeated cry of those who brings Job news of disaster: "And I only am escaped alone to tell thee." What, finally, does Ishmael wish to tell us?*

   To answer this question, first read the books of Jonah and Job in the Bible. Then reread carefully chapter 9, "The Sermon", and draw a conclusion as to Mapple's point about Jonah. Consider the more indirect use of Job in the novel, such as the quotation in the "Extracts", Ishmael calling Moby Dick "Job's whale" (see *Moby-Dick*, p. 234), and the epilogue's epigraph, as well as the whole theme in Job of why humans suffer. Then consider whether the novel as a whole bears out such biblical "lessons" or not.

3. *Consider the novel's many chapters on "whale matter"—facts and stories concerning whales and whaling. These begin with chapter 24, "The Advocate". Why is Ishmael so concerned with detailing all the world's knowledge about whales and whaling? How does this intermittent concentration on whales contribute to the book's themes about the quest for knowledge? Increasingly, Ishmael notes the many ironies and ambiguities associated with whales and whaling. In your discussion, consider at least several of these ironies and ambiguities and how Ishmael uses them analogically to point to some aspect of human life in the cosmos.*

First, draw a conclusion as to why Ishmael tries to detail every possible aspect of the whale for us. Consider this: after we know *everything* about the whale, what do we *really* know about the whale? What limits are there to human knowledge, and what is the proper response to this limitation? Then focus on one or more of the many chapters in which the ever-analogizing Ishmael pulls back from his minute descriptions of whale matter to make generalizations about human life. Some important chapters to consider are chapter 42, "The Whiteness of the Whale", and chapter 89, "Fast Fish and Loose Fish".

4. *Reread chapters 36 through 40, and also 46. Here, Ahab reveals his diabolical mission and rallies the crew's support. How does Ahab manage to muster his crew around his purpose by careful manipulation? What is the crew's response? Why do you suppose Melville begins here to present some chapters, such as 38, 39, and 40, like a play, with stage directions, soliloquies, and so forth?*

This question asks you to think deeply about Ahab's character and the fact that he has clearly preplanned every aspect of the Pequod's voyage to accomplish his own purposes. Consider how he does this as revealed in his own soliloquies (for example, chapter 37, "Sunset") and in Ishmael's musings on the matter (for example, chapter 46, "Surmises"—note that here as elsewhere, Ishmael tells us things a limited, first-person narrator cannot possibly know). How, in particular, does Ahab regard the crew—that is, other human beings—and what does the fact that he easily manipulates them say about weak human nature in the face of those who wield charismatic or tyrannical power?

5. *Note carefully the early chapters, such as chapter 10, "A Bosom Friend", and chapter 11, "Nightgown", where Ishmael and Queequeg form a close relationship, and later chapters that concern human affection, connection, and bonding, such as chapter 72 "The Monkey-rope", and chapter 94, "A Squeeze of the*

Hand". Read Nathaniel Hawthorne's short story "Ethan Brand" and then relate these chapters to (1) Hawthorne's conclusions in "Ethan Brand" about the "magnetic chain of humanity" and the consequences of separating oneself from it, and (2) Ahab's casting away of his pipe (chap. 30) and quadrant (chap. 118) and the successive loss of his "humanities" (see Moby-Dick, p. 118).

"Ahab has his humanities!" states Peleg to Ishmael. *Moby-Dick* reveals a man who is in some ways sympathetic to readers: Ahab has a wife and son, is compassionate to little Pip, and speaks with poignancy about his sufferings to Starbuck. But in order to pursue his quest, he consciously throws away those "humanities". Although apparently an unfinished piece, Hawthorne's "Ethan Brand" expresses issues that concerned Hawthorne all his writing life and were shared by Melville: the tragic—even diabolic—nature of cutting oneself off from one's brothers and sisters due to overweening pride. Describe how this theme can be seen in Captain Ahab's character development.

6. *Both before and during the Pequod's voyage, ominous signs and prophecies abound. Make a list of these and then choose several to explore in depth. What does the sign or prophecy point to, and why? How is it fulfilled in the Pequod's tragic end?*

There are, of course, many examples to choose from: for narrator Ishmael, numerous things on earth and in the heavens point to disaster. Here are just a few: Peter Coffin and the Spouter-Inn, the story of Jonah and Job, the prophet Elijah, the look of the Pequod, the significance of Ahab's name, Fedallah and the other stowaways, the terrifying myths surrounding Moby Dick, the "archangel" Gabriel, the fate of little Pip, Saint Elmo's fire, the reversing of the compass, and Fedallah's prophecy.

7. *Describe in full the three mates, Starbuck, Stubb, and Flask. What general type of humanity or kind of philosophy does each represent? Describe several scenes in which their given character traits are borne out.*

Begin with chapters 26 and 27, "Knights and Squires", and trace the characters of Starbuck, Stubb, and Flask, drawing a conclusion as to their consistency of portrayal. You may wish to combine this question with question 13 below, focusing most of your paper on Starbuck. (You may also wish to read Melville's famous short story "Bartleby the Scrivener" with its description of the three office workers Bartleby, Turkey, and Ginger-Nut, who, in a way, also represent "types" of humanity.)

8. *Beginning with chapter 52, "The Pequod meets the Albatross", a series of gams intersperse the narrative. Describe each gam in sequence. Discuss how each meeting bears on the main story at hand—Ahab and his monomaniacal quest for Moby Dick—and note any emerging pattern that appears throughout the gams. How, especially, does the final ship, the* Delight, *comment ironically on Father Mapple's sermon about "delight" and "woe" in chapter 9?*

Each gam might be said to give us more insight into the nature of Ahab and his quest. For example, "The Pequod meets the Albatross" provides yet another mounting instance of ominous occurrences as the ship closes in on its search for Moby Dick. Chapter 71, "The Pequod meets the Jeroboam. Her story" gives us an image of madness in the "archangel" Gabriel, who all but commands the ship and who prophesies disaster if the quest for the white whale is continued. Other gams show various reactions to Moby Dick that differ from Ahab's and thus call attention to Ahab's increasing monomania: for example. "The Pequod meets the Samuel Enderby of London". These are just a few examples to get you started in your thinking.

9. *Discuss Ahab as a tragic character, especially in his overweening pride and self-awareness.*

To answer this question, first look up the definition of a tragedy and a tragic character in a literary handbook. Consider whether Melville portrays Ahab as choosing his own fate or as completely determined by his circumstances. Consider also whether he accepts human limitations or seeks, in pride or hubris, to assert his dominance. Consider, finally, whether he is self-aware, understanding his actions and their consequences. You may wish to compare Ahab to other tragic heroes in such works as *Paradise Lost*, *Oedipus Rex*, and *King Lear*.

10. *Reread chapter 96, "The Try-Works". This chapter is often considered the climax or center of the book. What happens to Ishmael in this chapter, and what is his conclusion? What is Ishmael's point when he says that "there is a wisdom that is woe; but there is a woe that is madness" and mentions the "Catskill eagle" (see* Moby-Dick, *p. 495), and how do these conclusions relate to Ahab or the novel's themes as a whole? How do they relate to the theme developed by Solomon in the book of Ecclesiastes and to Father Mapple's sermon on "woe" versus "delight"?*

    Since Ishmael tells us here that "the truest of all men was the Man of Sorrows" and the "truest of all books is Solomon's, and Ecclesiastes is the fine hammered steel of woe", you need to read the book of Ecclesiastes and know about the life of Christ. Then concentrate on the last three paragraphs of chapter 96. Who in *Moby-Dick* suffers from an excessive amount of woe? Who from too much delight? In what way does Ishmael plead here for the *balanced* person, and how is this to be achieved? Note that much of Nathaniel Hawthorne's writing also suggests the need for such a "balanced" person versus one that "[l]ook[s] ... too long in the face of the fire" (see *Moby-Dick*, p. 494). You might read, as additional context, Hawthorne's "Young Goodman Brown", "The Minister's Black Veil", "Rappaccini's Daughter", "The Birthmark", or "Ethan Brand".

11. *Chapter 54, "The Town Ho's Story", is a long interpolated tale that Melville wrote for separate publication. In the figures of Steelkilt and Radney, how does the story provide a kind of microcosm of, or comment on, the tension between Starbuck and Ahab and the situation on the Pequod?*

This chapter is somewhat curious in the novel because here Ishmael recounts in detail a "potent" story he heard on the Pequod and that he later narrated in an inn in Lima (see *Moby-Dick*, p. 297). Nevertheless, although the style and form of this chapter is unique to the novel, "The Town Ho's Story" is yet another gam in the sequence of gams that involve the Pequod and thus has much to do with Ahab and his mission. Read the story of hatred, mutiny, and revenge carefully and note the tragic fate of Radney. Then compare and contrast the incidents in the story with the encounters between Starbuck and Ahab. Note that "The Town Ho's Story" tells us that Radney's hatred of Steelkilt is the innate antipathy of the ill-favored man for the handsome and noble man. One of Melville's most famous works, *Billy Budd*, also turns on this theme and would be worth your while to read as context.

12. *Along with his theme about the many contradictions and paradoxes of the universe, Melville dwells frequently in* Moby-Dick *on the subjectivity of human perception, that is, how it is often impossible to know the "truth" given that everyone has a different perception of that truth. Focus on chapter 99, "The Doubloon", in exploring this topic. What does each crew member see in the doubloon, and how does it reflect his personalities, philosophies, or goals?*

    Besides noting what each crew member sees in the doubloon and how his perceptions are borne out in his character, use other parts of the novel to illustrate how Ishmael continues to draw our attention to ambiguities or mysteries of life that lend themselves to multiple interpretations. Chapter 42, "The Whiteness of the Whale", is just one of many such passages. At the end of your paper, draw a conclusion as to what Melville is saying about the nature of truth and the limits of human knowledge.

13. *Describe in full the character of Starbuck, the first mate. To the last, he pleads with Ahab to cease the quest for Moby Dick. Trace his encounters with Ahab throughout the novel, and draw a conclu-*

sion as to why his *"mere unaided virtue" (see* Moby-Dick, *p. 234) is, finally, ineffective. Pay close attention to such moments as when Ahab gives in to him (chapter 109) and when Starbuck has a chance to kill or at least subdue Ahab and thus save the voyage (chapter 123). Is he right in not taking action against Ahab when he has the chance?*

This question is self-explanatory, asking you to do a close study of one of the most important characters in the novel—the only one who attempts to sway Ahab from his purpose. You may wish to combine this question with question 11 above; that is, you may wish to include a consideration of how chapter 54, "The Town Ho's Story", suggests the conflict between Starbuck and Ahab.

14. *According to the novel, is Ahab's diabolic quest determined by forces outside of him? Or does he have free will? To answer this question, consider all we know and see about Ahab throughout the novel. What choices does he consciously make, and why? In what ways does he consider his fate determined? What, finally, does Melville conclude about Ahab's culpability for the tragic end of the Pequod? Is Ahab a sympathetic character at all?*

As we see in many places, Ahab considers himself, as he states, "the Fates' lieutenant" (see *Moby-Dick*, p. 638), and he considers his mission one that he cannot alter. Yet at various times we see Ahab make conscious decisions and even consider alternatives to his actions. He is, in short, self-aware. Add up the evidence from both sides and draw a conclusion as to his culpability. In considering whether or not he is a sympathetic character, look at the reactions of others to him, especially that of Starbuck, Ishmael, and Pip.

15. *In the character of Captain Ahab,* Moby-Dick *seems to speak about the ruthlessness and destructive quality of total self-reliance and absolute exertion of power. It seems to indicate that one must strike a balance between "head" and "heart" and, for sanity's sake, remain connected with the rest of humanity. In what ways does Ishmael manage to do this? He tells us in chapter 1 that the story of Narcissus "is the key to it all" (see* Moby-Dick, *p. 31). What does he mean by this? You may also wish to consider how* Moby-Dick *responds to Emerson, Thoreau, and mid-nineteenth-century transcendental idealistic notions of self-reliance.*

This question is similar to question 5 above except that it asks you to concentrate on the character of Ishmael as the "balanced man" versus Ahab as the "monomaniac". In answering this question, note carefully such chapters as chapter 10, "A Bosom Friend", and chapter 11, "Nightgown", where Ishmael and Queequeg form a close relationship, and later chapters that concern human affection, connection, and bonding, such as chapter 72, "The Monkey-rope", and chapter 94, "A Squeeze of the Hand". How does the emphasis here on bonding with others counter the fate of Narcissus? Note also chapter 96, "The Try-Works", where Ishmael nearly succumbs to "inversion" by looking "too long in the face of the fire" (*Moby-Dick*, p. 494). As the question states, you would do well also to consider transcendental thought in such essays as Ralph Waldo Emerson's "Self-Reliance" and "Nature" or in Henry David Thoreau's *Walden*. Like Hawthorne, Melville responded to such idealism about human nature by insisting on what he calls "the power of blackness"—the strong force of evil in human nature and in the world. His review "Hawthorne and His Mosses", included in the Ignatius edition of *Moby-Dick*, will also be important for your discussion.

16. *One of* Moby-Dick's *themes concerns the limitation of human knowledge, especially in the face of the mysteries of the universe and of human suffering. Ahab states that he hates and hunts*

down the whale for its "inscrutable" aspect, that is, that which he cannot understand (see Moby-Dick, *p. 208). Ishmael, however, approaches the scope and limitation of human knowledge in a very different way, as revealed throughout the story he tells us. In what ways does Ishmael try to understand the mysteries of the universe and, in particular, the mysterious leviathan? What, by contrast, is Ahab's technique? Can the novel be said to contain a "moral" in regard to this theme?*

You might use the book of Job to frame your answer. In his suffering, Job attempts to probe God and God's ways. But when God shows up at the end of the book and answers Job, Job immediately backs away from his questions and says he's satisfied despite the fact that he really doesn't get an answer to his questions. Note carefully God's "answer" to Job and the implication that human knowledge must give way in humility and trust to God's mysteries. Then consider whether Melville is developing this theme in the novel.

17. *In what ways might the novel be considered an American epic? Comment, for example, on the work's use of American settings, characters, idiom, traditions, religion, history, and so forth, as well as the industry of whaling, to describe the universal; to describe how the novel mingles the spiritual or supernatural realm with the natural; and to describe how the Pequod, in its diverse crew and precarious sea voyage, represents a microcosm of all humanity.*

First, define a literary epic by consulting a good literary dictionary. Then add up all the elements of *Moby-Dick* that seem to respond to the idea of encapsulating an entire nation, its culture and mores and religion, its hopes and aspirations, in a fictional work. What does Melville gain by attempting an American epic?

18. *Through Ishmael,* Moby-Dick *frequently tells us that we must leave the shore and venture out to sea to be deep-thinking, fully alive people. "[B]etter is it to perish in that howling infinite,*

*than be ingloriously dashed upon the lee, even if that were safety!"
Ishmael tells us in the brief chapter on the fate of Bulkington
(chapter 23, "The Lee Shore"; see* Moby-Dick, *p. 147). But is
this true? Does the book—or, in your opinion, the more experienced Ishmael—still hold to this philosophy, given the novel's tragic end?*

Consider what the novel tells us about both the advantages and hazards of "deep diving" into life, a metaphor favored by Melville in describing the courage needed to plunge into life's challenges and mysteries. Consider also the development of Ishmael's character in regard to this "deep diving" from the beginning to the end of the novel.

Notes

Notes

Notes